School Today?
No
Way!

from
The **Happy** **Bappy** Collection

They called him Bappy
and he made people happy.

Before a day was done
and time came for sleep

It was a sure enough thing
that Bappy would creep

Into his bed
with a tired snout
from another day of helping out.

This day was going to be a
challenge.
THAT he could see.

By now the house should
be super quiet
with no-one within but he !

Something was different as far as
he could tell.

Because, at 9am, he should not be
hearing the voice of old Mrs Bell.
At least not if all is well.

Bappy lifted his head
from his cosy warm bed
to better hear
what was being said.

Some excitement was
occurring.

Was it really worth stirring?

Now what could be the
matter?
It is just the start of
another school day.

Indeed, a day that
should have been filled
with play.

That was according to a
young girl named Mo.

To school, she simply did not
want to go!!!

"I don't want to go" yelled eight
year old Mo

As she heard the bus
come over the hill.

"It's wet and it's cold and I'm far
too old."

"And I do not need to know what
I'm going to be told."

"Well"
said old Mrs Bell.

"What will you do if you don't go
to school?"

"Easy" said Mo.
"I'll discover new things all on
my own,
like making a call without a
mobile phone.

I'll invent things...

Like toys that dance,

Ponies that prance,

And clothes that doze...

Sounds like great fun
and there is much to
be done.

Now where should we start,
pondered the excited Mo.

She pulled out her
sketch book, her
colours and glue,

and then, she had no
idea what to do.

Maybe eat an apple and
draw a chocolate muffin?

OR draw an apple
and eat a chocolate
muffin?

"Whatever" said Old Mrs
Bell admiring the muffin.

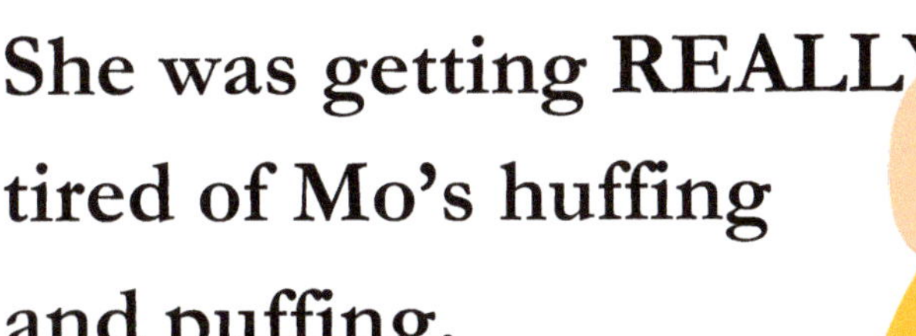

She was getting REALLY
tired of Mo's huffing
and puffing.

Aside from eating
that muffin,
Mrs Bell came up with
absolutely nothing!

She was 82.
She didn't know
what to do.
She didn't know how
to get Mo
to just go!

Mrs Bell decided
to help out Mo
by calling in
Grandma Jo.

Grandma Jo is very smart.
Chances are that Mo will soon
have a big change of heart.

"Indeed" said Grandma Jo.
I'll soon have this one out to
school on her tippy toes.

"Now let's get going"
said Jo.

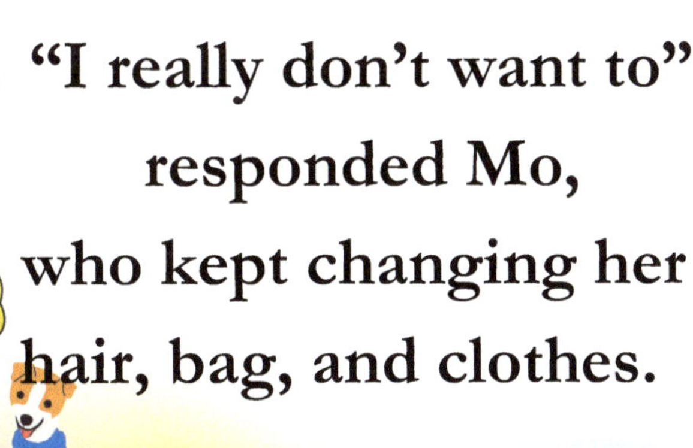

"I really don't want to"
responded Mo,
who kept changing her
hair, bag, and clothes.

Oh dear, oh dear.
Now, what's a grandma to do
here?

"I know" said
Jo to Mo.

"You're tired
and blue,

but it's the end
of the week

so off to school
with you!"

"I simply refuse to go"
said the now fairly bold Mo.

This was an unexpected
challenge for Grandma Jo.

"Oh dear, oh dear,
what am I going to do here"
said Grandma Jo to herself
as she pulled apart every shelf.

She could teach her guitar, do
puzzles....

 ... read a book

...or learn chess.

Whatever it is, Jo will always do her best!"

"Ok Mo,
let us begin with the
very first thing"
said Jo.

When Mo saw
the guitar
she wanted to run very far.

A look of disgust
spread over her face.

Grandma Jo got
the same response
to almost everything she said.

Jo was now stuck like
glue.

She couldn't think of
anything new.
So,
what was she to do?

Mo just would not go to
school today. Mo told Jo,
"School today?
No way!".

Jo was getting tired,
her patience had
been tried.

Then, out of the blue, Jo
yelled out......

Mo yelled back even louder

N O!

It didn't look like anything
was going to change
apart from Mo's clothes
and she had a fairly big range.

She had clothes on racks,

She had clothes
in stacks,

She had clothes
on the floor,

She had
clothes
on the door,

and in the laundry
basket, she had
even more!

On top of all these
clothes, she had a
huge colletion of
ribbons and bows.

In addition to all that,
she had many scarves,
hairslides, and
even hair extensions!

All of which,
was now causing
a fair amount of tension.

Suddenly, Mo announced
to the adults in a very
grown up tone,
"I've had enough of this
rubbish".

Cheeky as can be,
a big smile spread over her face
and off she went on her bike
at an almighty pace!

"I'm going to see Kay, the local
DJ" she called back to Jo,
who did not know which way to go.

By now, Mrs Bell was under
a muffin spell,

and Grandma Jo still didn't know
which way to go.

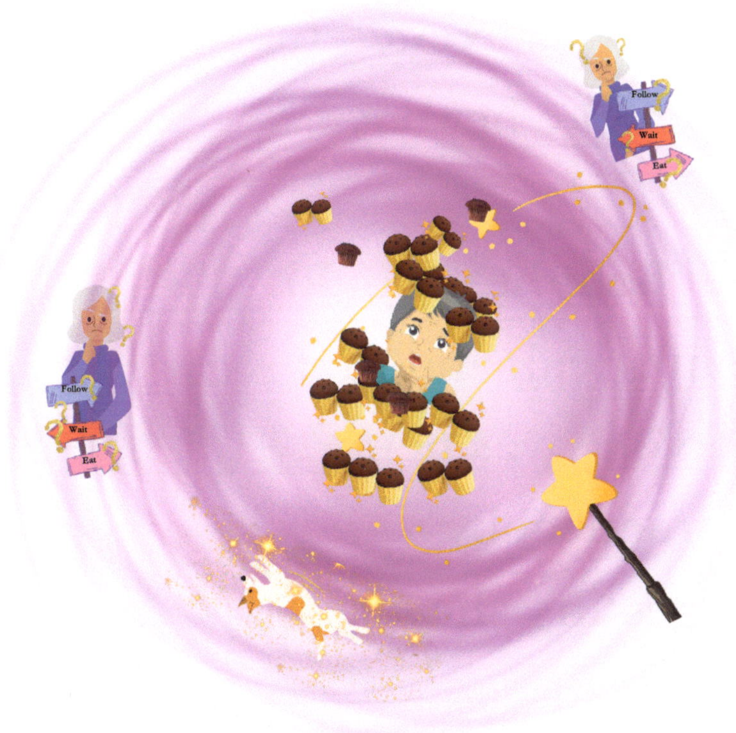

They were both 82!
They **SHOULD** know what to do!

Mo had imagined a
fantastic day,
full of fun,
dress up,
and general play.

Bappy was excited to
help make her day.

She thought it would
be magical, and that
everyone was being
impractical by
suggesting she was
just theatrical.

Off she went, full speed ahead
towards Ballintuss.

Then suddenly the front
door flew open wide.

And all of a sudden,
Mo was back inside
And wanted to hide.

The time was gone past one
And the Friday school day was
already done

It soon became clear to
Mrs Bell and Jo
what had caused such a panic
with the brazen Mo.

Of all the people she thought
were chill
Number One was
Grandpa Bill
and here he was now
driving the bus
back over the hill.

Mo had forgotten all about
Bill being the
fill-in driver of the bus
to her school in Ballintuss.

That explains him
leaving early
this morning
full of cheer.

He loved being
a fill-in driver
at this time of year.

But for Mo
this day was turning bad.

She was getting
very sad.

Bill will ask,
"how was your day?"

Now she had no idea
what to say.

What can
she say that she did
with her day?

No-show Mo.
Missed relaxing
yoga class.

No-show Mo.
Replaced as
concert organiser.

No-show Mo.
Missed
field explorer walk.

Mo had just wanted a day of fun.
But now the house was
upside down
with three half-crazy adults sitting
around.

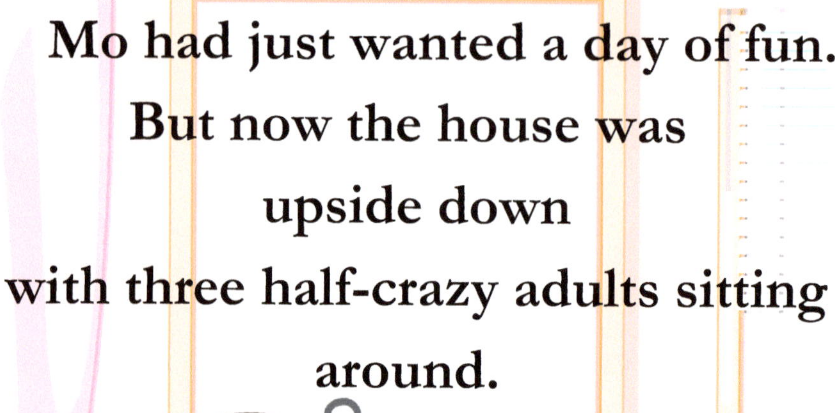

Not wanting to speak or even
say good night.

She sat on her bed
feeling full of dread
with an increasingly
painful pain in her head.

By now she should be
sound asleep.
But instead she found
her worries run deep.

She replayed the day over and
over as she lay there in bed.

By missing school,
Who did she make
mad?

Who did she
make sad?

Was everybody now thinking she
was just all bad?

Her head hurt.

Her eyes were alert.

Until she heard the tapping of feet that were small coming down the hall.

She got distracted from her thoughts and found her head became a little less sore.

As the sound of feet got closer, she got distracted a little bit more.

She looked up
and saw Bappy
waiting at the door.

This made her
forget another
bit more.

Bappy entered the
room and sat beside
her on the floor.

Now Mo forgot a
whole lot more!

She reached down her
hand to stroke his fine
hair

And now her horrible
thoughts were getting a
lot less care.

On seeing this change,
Bappy decided to stay
right there.

Mo's actions of the day had
made her feel sad.

Bappy's presence helped
her to stop feeling so bad.

Come Monday, she would
go to school, standing
proud and tall.

Maybe even join a club and
play some ball.

Now her thoughts were focused on new adventures.

Her eyes became weary and tiredness crept over her clearly.

She pulled the duvet up to her chin and threw all her woes into the bedside bin.

Her head grew light with the thought of the sleep she would have that night.

"One last thing"
she whispered gently to Bappy.
"Thank you and good night."

As this day was done and
it was now time for sleep,
Mo saw Bappy creep
into his bed with a tired snout
from another day of helping out.

He closed his eyes and
settled his head
as he sank down deep
into his safe and peaceful bed.

Goodnight
Bappy.

9 781036 903572